A DAY IN THE LIFE OF A
NATIVE AMERICAN

Emma Helbrough

Illustrated by Inklink, Firenze

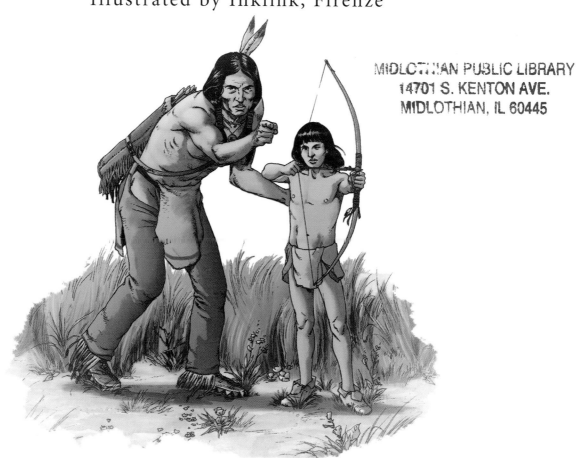

PowerKiDS
press.

New York

Published in 2008 by The Rosen Publishing Group, Inc.
29 East 21st Street, New York, NY 10010

Created and produced by Emma Godfrey, Emma Helbrough, Rachel Coombs, Nicholas Harris and Sarah Hartley, Orpheus Books Ltd.

Consultant: Dr Sam Maddra, Department of History, University of Glasgow

Library of Congress Cataloging-in-Publication Data

Helbrough, Emma
A day in the life of a Native American / Emma Helbrough.
p. cm. — (A day in the life)
Includes index.
ISBN-13: 978-1-4042-3854-1 (lib. bdg.)
ISBN-10: 1-4042-3854-9 (lib. bdg.)
1. Indians of North America—Juvenile literature. I. Title.
E77.4.H45 2008
970.004'97—dc22

2007002908

Manufactured in Malaysia.

CONTENTS

ABOUT THIS BOOK

In this captivating book you will follow a very busy day in the life of a Native American living on the North American plains during the 19th century. Along the way, you will learn about what life was like for the Native Americans, from the food they ate to the battles they fought.

This is Tall Wolf. He is the main character in this story.

Look out for these questions. Answers are on page 31.

TELLING THE TIME

There is a clock in the corner of each page, so you can check what time it is in the story, but in truth the Native Americans did not use clocks like this one. They thought of time in a different way. They ate when they were hungry, rose when the sun came up and slept when it went down.

LIFE IN NORTH AMERICA

The Native American people first arrived in North America from Asia many thousands of years ago. They quickly spread out across the continent, forming different tribes, each with its own customs and language.

A tribe's way of life depended on the area it settled in. Some tribes settled on the open plains in the West and hunted buffalo, while others lived in the deserts in the Southwest, where they gathered seeds and grew crops. In the vast woodlands in the East, people hunted deer and gathered berries, while in the frozen lands of the Far North, they hunted seals and caught fish.

During the 16th century, Europeans began to arrive in North America and settled on the East Coast. By the 19th century, the European population had expanded greatly. They began forcing Native Americans off their land, claiming it as their own. Most Native Americans did not want to leave their homelands and fought bitterly against the American government.

Native Americans searching for buffalo on the North American Plains.

TRAVELING

It is six o'clock in the morning and Tall Wolf's Sioux Indian tribe is moving camp, following the route of the migrating buffalo herd across the North American plains. The animals provide the tribe with clothes and shelter as well as food, so it is important that they stay close to the herd.

All of their possessions are secured to travois, sleds that are attached to their horses' backs.

Riding at the front of the group with his son, Little Crow, Tall Wolf looks for a good spot to set up camp. It must have plenty of fresh water, firewood, and good grass for their horses to graze on.

SETTING UP CAMP

Tall Wolf has found a perfect spot for his tribe. There are scattered trees nearby, but the area is open, so there is little chance for warriors from an enemy tribe to ambush their camp.

The women begin unloading their travois and putting up tepees. First they make a wooden frame, tying the poles together with a rope made of leather. Then they cover the frame with buffalo hides sewn together.

Fact or Fiction?

Native Americans wore feathers in their hair.

DAILY TASKS

Once the camp is fully set up, the women begin their daily chores. Some explore the plains, gathering berries and fruits, such as wild strawberries and juicy plums. They pick peppermint and other herbs, too, which will flavor their cooking.

Back at camp, Tall Wolf's wife, Plenty Blankets, is draping strips of buffalo meat over a rack to dry in the hot sun. Once dried, the meat will keep for several months and will feed the tribe during the difficult winter months when food becomes scarce.

Two women have stretched out a buffalo hide and pegged it to the ground.

They are scraping a layer of fat off the surface, using a tool made of bone. When it has been scraped clean, they will turn it over and scrape off the hair. Then they will soften it by rubbing the surface with boiled and liquefied buffalo brains. The finished hide will be made into clothes, shoes, called moccasins, or a tepee cover.

While the women go about their work, Tall Wolf spends some time with his son, teaching him how to shoot with a bow and arrow. At the moment Little Crow is shooting at a still target on a tree, but with a little more practice he will be ready to shoot at wild rabbits and other small animals.

Fact or fiction?

All Native Americans lived in tepees.

SCOUTING BUFFALO

Now it is mid-morning, and Tall Wolf is preparing for today's hunt. Along with two other hunters, Blue Horse and Standing Cloud, he leaves camp to search for the buffalo herd. The scouts travel on horseback, shielding their eyes from the sun so they can see far across the plains. Sometimes it only takes hours to locate the herd, but other times it can take days, so they need to stay alert.

As they near the top of a hill, the men dismount and cautiously approach the edge. They stay low to the ground in case the buffaloes or enemies from a rival tribe are in sight.

Peering over the hill, they see the herd wandering across the plains, following the curve of the river.

Tall Wolf is relieved to find the herd so soon. He gives thanks to the spirits for guiding them to the animals. Then he signals to Blue Horse and Standing Cloud to head back to camp, where they can announce the good news to everyone. They will gather together the rest of the hunting party and return.

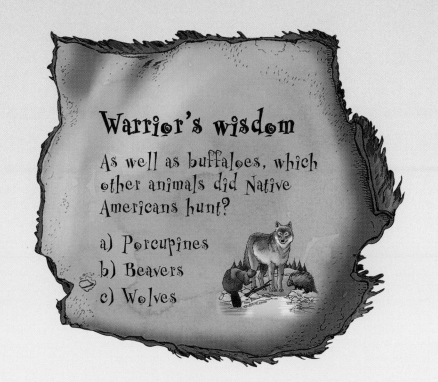

Warrior's wisdom

As well as buffaloes, which other animals did Native Americans hunt?

a) Porcupines
b) Beavers
c) Wolves

HUNTING

Tall Wolf and Blue Horse are now galloping alongside the buffalo herd as it thunders across the open plains. A buffalo can easily topple and crush a horse and rider to death during a stampede, so the hunters use their great riding skills to dodge the powerful beasts.

Tall Wolf sees that one of the animals—an older male—is already tiring and a gap is starting to form between it and the other buffaloes. He cuts in beside the beast to separate it fully from the herd. Now he will be able to get a clear shot at the animal. Tall Wolf draws back his bow and fires at the buffalo's thick side. It topples to the floor and lies still.

The men dismount from their horses to give thanks to the spirits and to the dead animal, which they believe has sacrificed itself so that they can live.

15

FEASTING

The tribe gathers at the site of the kill for a feast, prepared by the women. The men eat the animal's raw liver first, as they believe it will bring them great strength and courage in hunting and battles. Tall Wolf and Blue Horse are given the animal's tongue, a real delicacy, as a reward for their successful hunt.

The women begin making a stew. They heat rocks in a fire and then drop them into a pot of water with some chunks of meat, fresh turnips, and herbs. It soon begins to bubble.

Tall Wolf eats until he can manage no more. There is still plenty of food left, but nothing goes to waste. The meat will be cut into strips and dried.

TRADING

It is now three o'clock and Tall Wolf is visiting another tribe's camp to trade goods. The Mandan Indians are farmers, not hunters like the Sioux.

They grow crops such as corn and beans. Today Tall Wolf is trading buffalo hides for the Mandans' corn.

The two tribes are wary of each other, but they always remain polite and courteous for these meetings.

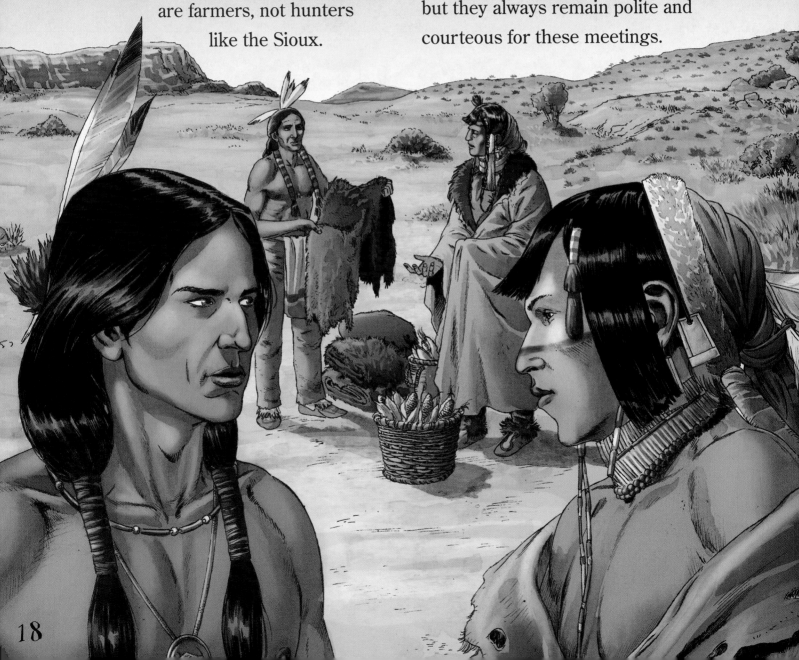

They recognize that trading is very useful to them both. It also provides an opportunity to share stories, ideas, and news. The two tribes speak different languages, but they are able to communicate well with hand gestures and facial expressions.

The Mandans have bad news. They have discovered a white settlement on the edge of Sioux territory. The settlers have built a house there and fenced off the land so they can keep cattle and grow crops.

Warrior's wisdom

How did Native Americans measure their wealth?

a) The size of their tepee
b) How many horses they had
c) How much food they had

Tall Wolf feels angry when he learns this. The white men have no right to settle in their territory. By doing so they are waging war on the Sioux. Tall Wolf thanks the Mandans and then hastily heads back to camp to break the bad news to everyone.

This is not the first time the Sioux have heard of white settlers. More and more of them have been arriving on the plains. Tall Wolf feels sad, but he is sure that their chief will know what to do.

19

COUNCIL

Back at camp, chief Red Hawk calls a meeting in the council tepee for all the warriors. The men wear their formal buffalo robes and sit around a fire, solemnly smoking a ceremonial pipe. Each man's shield is hung above his seat. As they inhale the smoke, they ask the spirits for help in making war with the white settlers.

Afterwards they discuss what should be done. Only one man talks at a time, as is the polite way, while the others listen and nod. Everyone is agreed that they must try to force the white men off their land. They have no right to be there. Chief Red Hawk suggests they should charge the settlement to show their anger and frighten the settlers away.

PREPARING FOR WAR

The warriors begin preparing for battle. Only the men will go to war, as they are the protectors of the tribe. They gather their bows and arrows and sharpen their spears and tomahawks.

To their hair and shields they attach medicine bundles, which contain sacred things belonging to the owner, such as seed pods, animal teeth, or quartz crystals. The warriors believe these will bring them strength and bravery in battle.

Next they paint their shields, bodies, and horses with markings to show their achievements in battles and protective symbols of animals and the spirit world. Tall Wolf uses a brush made of porcupine-tail hair and paints colored with moss and plant pigments. Fully prepared, the men are an imposing sight to behold.

22

Finally, the warriors visit the tribe's medicine man, or shaman, to receive his blessing before the battle. He performs a ceremonial dance, asking the spirits to bring them great success.

Fact or fiction?

Native Americans greeted each other by saying "how."

23

ATTACK!

It does not take long for Tall Wolf and the warriors to find the settlement. The Mandans have described its location well. They charge towards the homestead and begin circling it on horseback, shooting a stream of arrows at the windows.

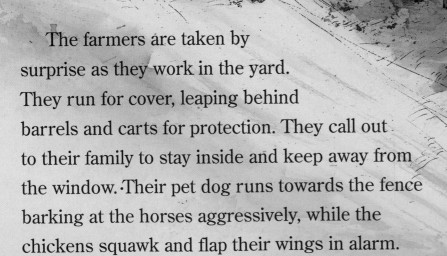

The farmers are taken by surprise as they work in the yard. They run for cover, leaping behind barrels and carts for protection. They call out to their family to stay inside and keep away from the window. Their pet dog runs towards the fence barking at the horses aggressively, while the chickens squawk and flap their wings in alarm.

The farmers grab shotguns and begin firing at the Indians, but the warriors are skilled riders as well as fighters. They quickly slip down the side of their saddles to avoid being hit. Then they are straight back up again, making loud war cries as they shoot more arrows at the homestead. Seeing the fear on the farmers' faces is enough for Tall Wolf. He realizes the Indians have made their point and signals to the others to return to camp.

Fact or fiction?

Native Americans danced around totem poles.

GREAT WELCOME

The whole tribe rushes out to greet the men on their return. Everyone is thankful that noone was hurt during the battle. The Sioux do not believe in great

bloodshed during warfare. Their aim was simply to protect their people and show their bravery. Tall Wolf recounts what happened in great detail. The children gather around him to listen in awe. Some of them re-enact the scenes with imaginary weapons. Little Crow beams proudly at his brave warrior father.

WAR DANCE

The evening is filled with joyful festivities. The tribe has two things to celebrate: the successful hunt and the victorious battle. The warriors begin the celebrations with a war dance to thank the great spirits of the sky for bringing them help.

In a trancelike state they circle the fire, singing and swaying rhythmically. In their hair they wear eagle feathers, each one marking an achievement in a past battle.

Chief Red Hawk wears his impressive war bonnet as a sign of his great courage and bravery. After the dance, they sit under the stars, telling the folktales their grandfathers told them. Tall Wolf feels a great contentment. The war with the white settlers may not be over yet, but, just at this moment, life is good.

GLOSSARY

ere you can check the meaning of some of the words in this book.

ambush (am-BUSH) To jump out from a hidden place and attack without warning.

buffalo hide (BUH-fuh-loh HYD) The skin of a buffalo.

buffalo robe (BUH-fuh-loh ROHB) A buffalo hide with the hair left on the outside for extra warmth.

ceremonial pipe (ser-eh-MOH-nee-ul PYP) A pipe smoked during solemn rituals.

homestead (HOHM-sted) A house built by early white settlers on the plains.

medicine bundle (MEH-duh-sun BUN-dul) A wrapped-up bundle of sacred objects, which the Native Americans believed would bring special powers to the owner.

moccasins (MAH-kuh-sunz) Shoes made of soft buffalo leather.

plains (PLAYNZ) Large areas of grasslands and hills which cover central North America.

shaman (SHAH-mun) A medicine man with healing and spiritual powers.

spirits (SPIR-uts) Supernatural forces that Native Americans believed controlled things on Earth.

stampede (stam-PEED) When a large group of animals suddenly rushes forward.

tepee (TEE-pee) A house made of buffalo hides stretched over a frame.

totem pole (TOH-tem POHL) A wooden pole carved with animals and mythical creatures, which symbolizes a family's history.

travois (truh-VOY) A sled used to transport goods across the plains.

tribe (TRYB) A group of people that live together as a community.

war dance (WOR DANTS) A ritual dance that warriors performed after a successful battle to thank the spirits for their help.

ANSWERS

Page 8 – Fact! Brave warriors wore feathers in their hair to show their achievements in battles.

Page 11 – Fiction! Only tribes that hunted buffaloes lived in tepees. Other tribes lived in homes made of grass, bark, and other materials.

Page 13 – a and b. Porcupine quills were used for sewing and weaving. Beavers were hunted for their skin, which was believed to have special healing powers, and their teeth, which were made into necklaces. Wolves were rarely hunted.

Page 17 – Fact! Warriors painted their faces and bodies with spiritual symbols to protect them in battle.

Page 19 – b. Horses were a tribe's most valuable possession and every rider had a special bond with his horse. Warriors even went on horse-stealing raids to steal horses from rival tribes. This often resulted in revenge attacks and even full-blown wars.

Page 23 – Fiction! Each tribe spoke a different language, so each had its own greeting.

Page 25 – Fiction! Only Native Americans on the northwest coast built totem poles, and they were not for dancing around. They were monuments which recorded a family's history.

Page 29 – a and c. Native American children did not go to school, but boys learned how to hunt and fight, while girls practiced cooking, crafts, and preparing hides. There was plenty of time for playing games too.

INDEX